THE ULTIMATE GUIDE IN OVERCOMING EXCUSES

TAKE THE 30 DAYS NO EXCUSE CHALLENGE AND CHANGE YOUR LIFE FOREVER

WILLIAM CAPERS JR

WHY YOU SHOULD READ THIS BOOK

NO MORE EXCUSES! It is time to take responsibility for your life. No matter how bad things have been – FOCUS on what you can do NOW to make it better. What action can you take NOW to ensure your life will be better in the future?
In this book you are going to learn how to overcome all common excuse so you can live a better life.

Table of Contents

I DON'T WANT TO SPEND TOO MUCH TIME AWAY FROM MY FAMILY

I AM TOO TIRED

I DID EVERYTHING YOU COULD

INTRODUCTION

Do you make excuses or take initiative?

Okay, we've all been there. Something just doesn't work out, or something doesn't quite go the way you had expected. Just maybe you failed to hit the target you had in mind.

When things don't quite pan out as you had imagined, do you typically take ownership? Do you take responsibility? Maybe you're the kind of person who takes initiative? Or maybe you are the kind of person who just makes excuses?

Yep, excuses are great. After all they make us feel much better about ourselves. Making excuses means that it's easier to live with our failed expectations. As a bonus, we win the sympathy of others, which in turn helps us to create deeper bonds with those around us. We're not perfect after all, in fact we are quite flawed and achieving our goals and objectives is tough work. Excuses provide us with reasons that help us explain away why we just aren't good enough.

Many of us have big dreams and aspirations. This is of course wonderful. However, the reality is that many people don't end up achieving the big goals they set for themselves. And it's not that people aren't capable. Many of us are more than capable of achieving things beyond our wildest imaginations, however for most, this never actually becomes a reality because people just kind of get in their own way.

The way we kind of get in our own way comes through the excuses we consistently make for not having enough, for not achieving a goal, for not handling a problem, or for not making the most of the opportunities life throws our way.

All these excuses keep us stuck. They keep us stuck in limbo. We want all these wonderful things, but unfortunately for most people... well, they will actually never have them. We won't have these wonderful things because the excuses we make prevent us from moving forward.

Success of course isn't a straight line moving from Point A to B. In reality this line zigzags, weaves, loops, and even knots up at times. There is still a Point A and B, however getting there takes a lot more work than what most of us probably expected when we first set out on this journey toward accomplishing our goals.

The unpredictable nature of this path means that we will experience many roadblocks and obstacles that temporarily prevent us from moving forward.

During these moments you can either take initiative and commit yourself to plowing through these challenges, or you can sit back, relax and make excuses as to why you simply couldn't make any progress.

It's these excuses we make that keep most people living in mediocrity. Instead of taking ownership and responsibility for the situation they find themselves in, they prefer to simply wilt under the pressure and accept defeat before the final buzzer has even sounded.

These people just don't have enough drive, dedication or motivation to push themselves forward. As a result they resign to the fact that life will never be the way they had always imagined.

What if instead of making excuses these people dedicated themselves to just simply plowing forward along their journey? What if they had no option but to move forward irrelevant of the obstacles that life threw their way? What if making excuses brought upon them incredible shame and humiliation? What then? Would they still make these same excuses? Or would they simply dig deeper and push themselves further?

These are all interesting scenarios. Making excuses is just easy. In fact, people feel much better about themselves after an excuse because it just helps them make peace with their failed expectations. However, as good as it feels, it doesn't change anything. In fact, their excuses just keep them stuck, and in the long-run they end up feeling miserable as excuses turn into regrets of a life that could have been lived.

The only way you will ever get to that place you have imagined in your mind's-eye — where all your goals and dreams have become a reality — is by letting go of all your excuses. This means giving up on all the things you say to yourself as to why you couldn't, shouldn't, didn't or wouldn't do something. It also means taking ownership, responsibility and initiative to move forward with purpose. In fact, taking initiative is the polar opposite of making excuses. When you take initiative to work through something, there are no excuses to be made. You just accept everything and you do whatever needs to get done to move yourself forward.

This is of course all well and good, however letting go of our excuses isn't always easy. It ain't easy because many of the excuses we make are habitual by nature. We make excuses about certain things because we've always made these kinds of excuses. It's just easy to make them, and changing our habits takes work and effort.

The excuses we make are also tied to our belief systems. We believe certain things about ourselves, about others and/or about life, and these beliefs then manifest as excuses as to why we couldn't or didn't do something. Many of these beliefs are of course irrational. They are based on circumstantial evidence that may or may not apply to every situation. And in some cases these beliefs are just downright absurd and have no basis in reality.

Now lets explore some of the common excuses that people typically make and discuss how to counteract them. In other words, let's identify these excuses and then figure out what you can do to overcome them.

I DON'T HAVE ENOUGH RESOURCES

One of the most famous mistakes people fall in when trying to set goals is thinking that they should have all the resources that enables them to reach the goal before they can set the goal.

By thinking that way those people end up choosing goals that are smaller than the ones they wanted to achieve. They may be thinking that they are being more realistic but the truth is that they are wrong. After all if you have all of the resources that can make you reach what you want then there is no need for goal setting.

"Set the Goals first and the Resources will Come Next"

By setting the goals first you will be giving an order to your subconscious mind to start to seek possible ways of reaching it. Even if you gave your mind a goal that seems out of your reach it will do its best to find new ways to reach it.

If your subconscious mind believed that you can't reach something then it wont bother show you the way to do it as a result of believing that there is no hope. If you convinced your subconscious mind that you really want to get that thing then the search mode will be activated and your mind will start to attract ideas that can help you in reaching these goals.

DON'T CONSTRAIN YOUR POTENTIAL

By setting the goal first you wont be putting any constrains on your abilities while if you just counted the resources that you have then set your goals then you will end up with a list of goals that is much humbler than your true potential.

Success Vs excuses

I was attending a lecture with a famous millionaire who was teaching us how to make money. During the lecture she paused and said: Some people make money while others make excuses.

Its up to you whether you really want to change your life or whether you just want to find an excuse that makes you feel less guilty.

Even if your excuses worked after some time the lie will come to the surface and you will feel really bad. Compare this to taking responsibility of your life and to making your dreams come true!

I DON'T HAVE ENOUGH EXEPERIENCE

I just don't have enough experience to pull this off.

I'm just not quite ready yet.

This one's for the credential junkie (i.e. John Smith MBA, CP3, MTV, BET, TALK, ETC.). Some people think they don't have enough experience, so they worry themselves into not living their dreams. These people are basically saying, "I'm not good enough."

I've also seen people settle for far less. Year after year, they work for minimal compensation without even considering that they are good enough to get paid more. Frankly, we all have experience. It's called 'life experience.' We can use this for any kind of work we are involved with.

Instead of making this excuse, commit yourself to taking very small but gradual steps toward your desired objective. You don't necessarily need to even know or understand all the steps of the process you are taking. All you have to know is what needs to happen next, right here and right now. Everything else will come to light as soon as you start moving forward. And above all else, remember that there is always a first time for everyone and for everything. We all start with baby steps before we learn to run.

THERE IS TIME FOR EVERYTHING

"Do not wait: the time will never be 'just right'. Start where you stand, and work with whatever tools you may have at your command and better tools will be found as you go along."— Napoleon Hill

There is never a perfect time for you to take action. There is never a perfect time for you to launch that project, to spend time with your family, to write a book, change your habit, or embrace a new habit. Once you acknowledge this, you will get a lot more meaningful work done everyday.
Kill the excuses!

"The only thing standing between you and your goal is the bullshit story you keep telling yourself as to why you can't achieve it." — Jordan Belfort

I'm too tired. I don't have the time. I am not capable. Someone else will do it. It's too late now. Now is not the right time. I am not talented. I am not ready. I'm too scared. Nobody will help me. What if I fail. I don't feel motivated. I'd rather do nothing. I don't have the money..yet!

It's easy to come up with excuses and justify not getting started. The longer you fill your head with rationalizations and empty excuses, the less time you have to take action.

It's easy to say, "I will start when I have more experience, money, time and resources". By this time next year, you will have a lot more excuses. It's a cycle. And once you get caught in the loop, it, can be difficult to break free and do something meaningful you care about.

Many people are living their entire lives without ever standing up and stepping out. But it's exciting to witness the rare few who dare themselves and step out of their personal bubbles to make a change.

Most of use live with the stubborn illusion that we will always have tomorrow to do today's work. We consistently hold on to this belief and keep procrastinating until work becomes a heavy burden.

Left unchecked, we always default toward a more comfortable path. Your comfortable zone provides a state of mental security. You can understand why it's so hard to kick your brain out of your comfort zone.
It pays to be an outlier!

"Outliers are those who have been given opportunities—and who have had the strength and presence of mind to seize them."—Malcom Gladwell

Outliers are those who seize opportunities and run with them. People who realize how little time they have and are driven to make the absolute most of it. Those are the ones who really live.

Studies consistently show that when we look back on our lives the most common regrets are not the risks we took, but the ones we didn't. Of the many regrets people describe, regrets of inaction outnumber those of action by nearly two to one.

Some of the most common include not being more assertive, and failing to seize the moment. When people reflect later in life, it is the things they did not do that generate the greatest despair. You can seize the moment today!
Getting past the biggest hurdle!

The biggest hurdle for many of us is simply getting started. Making that important decision to take a step. You can be as big and successful as you can possibly imagine if you build that mindset you need to step outside the safe zone. You just don't trust yourself enough yet.

You have everything you need to make an impact in the world if you can get past the excuses. You don't even have to start a new project. What you need is something you can emotionally and deeply connect with.

Don't think too far into the future. Use what you have right now at where you are and witness the magic of creative work. If you're thinking about it too much, chances are you're killing it.
Get started now!

"It is better to live your own destiny imperfectly than to live an imitation of somebody else's life with perfection." — Anonymous, The Bhagavad Gita

No matter who you are or what you dream of becoming, remember this: No one ever came to this planet to take a back seat, play second fiddle or make it small.

Stop questioning yourself. Stop listening to everyone else. The world is waiting for you to start something. Waiting to hear what you have to say. Waiting to use your creative product or service. Waiting to share your ideas and original work.

Remember the dream you were too scared to chase? It's still not too late to give it a try. We tend to think that we're not good enough, and give up before we even start. The fear of taking risks never goes away but it does become familiar.

The self-criticism and self-doubt will always be present, and the only solution is to just act in spite of them. Your first ebook, article, song, podcast, freelancer work or creative work never will not be satisfying and perfect, and it's okay.

When we express ourselves in a way that brings out the best in us, we've already succeeded. Step by step we improve despite the temporary failures. That's what matters. It matters that you persist.

"Don't wait until everything is just right. It will never be perfect.

There will always be challenges, obstacles and less than perfect conditions.

So what. Get started now. With each step you take, you will grow stronger and stronger, more and more skilled, more and more self-confident and more and more successful." — *Mark Victor Hansen*

Take advantage of the enormous opportunities the information age presents. You have everything you need to go make something meaningful. Something you deeply care about. You don't have to be right when you start. But it matters that you begin now.

There isn't a right time for anything. There's no such thing as perfect timing. If it feels right, just go for it today. Don't wait until everything is just perfect or right. Get started now.

GOD HAS A PLAN FOR ME

"God's plan for you can only materialize when you dutifully align yourself with it."
-William Capers

One of the things that God hates is idleness. Not only does it bring poverty, but it brings shame, hunger, disappointment, ruin, and more sin in your life. Have you ever heard the phrase idle hands are the devil's workshop?

No biblical leader had anything to do with the sin of idleness. If a man is not willing to work he will not eat. We should never be overworking ourselves and we all need sleep, but too much sleep will hurt you.

I task these words sometimes because in most part world, many people use God as a protection for keeping idle. Your responsibility is totally yours.God won't arranged goals for you, research for you, tell you what to do, go to places foryou, build associations for you, take up a company for you, earn a living for you, or even write a book for you.

Trusting God is wise. In fact, that's about the most wise thing you could do.

Proverbs tells us

Trust in the Lord with all your heart and lean not on your own understanding; in all your ways submit to him, and he will make your paths straight. – Proverbs 3:5-6

Reading this passage, you might find yourself blindly trusting and resting in laziness. You might be tempted to trust, but not work. To trust, but not plan. To trust, but not structure and create systems.

But what's often overlooked here is that trusting God doesn't exempt us from having "ways." The verse says, "In all your ways..." which presumes even in trusting you'll create plans and systems and organizations. That you'll evaluate, create infrastructures, and plan forward. In this process, if we choose to submit every detail to God, trusting Him first, he'll make our paths straight.

Not "straight" in that everything will be successful as we often define success. But "straight" in that our ways can honor God.

I DON'T KNOW THE RIGHT PEOPLE

I just don't know the right people.

I don't know anyone who could help me get ahead.

If you don't know the right people, start networking. Instead of making this excuse, be more proactive with developing deeper relationships and connections with those around you. Attend networking events, join mastermind groups, and ask to be introduced to people who you would like to get to know. The key here is to go the extra mile to meet, greet and connect with people. As you expand your social and professional network you will eventually get to know people who can help you to get ahead.

if we believe in ourselves, none of these things have to deter us. As we do what we love and create new possibilities for ourselves, we will inevitably form mutually beneficial relationships.

In my early days on Twitter, I had a different account where I tweeted uplifting messages. It was my first attempt at making the difference I wanted to make.

Back then, I'd never have imagined I'd be connected to so many amazing people, and I wasn't sure I could run a website, since I knew nothing about the tech side of things.

One day, a cotent developer named John wesley tweeted about me, complimenting my profile and tweets. Since we connected then, he's been a huge help with the site, and he's become one of my closest confidantes, consultants, and friends.

There are countless people out there who could support and help us, but we can only meet them if we put ourselves out there too.

I HAVE TRIED IT BEFORE IT DIDN'T WORK

I've tried and it just can't be done.

This is an outright lie at times. People use this to get out of situations and to avoid things they just don't feel like doing. Some people say this just to prove their point to someone. Obese people sometimes use this to avoid dieting.

I've tried and failed... I give up!

Instead of making this excuse, reach out to someone for help, guidance and assistance. Other people may have more experience in this situation, or may have gone through this process a little differently that you. Pick their brains and learn everything you can from them, then adjust your course of action moving forward. And if help isn't available, then ask yourself:

If it was possible, how could it be done?

There is always a way, you just need to find it. Sometimes all it takes is a slight shift in your perspective.

NOBODY BELIEVES IN ME

"belief in youself and all that you are. Know that there is something greater inside you than any obstacle"

Nobody believes that I can do this.

Everyone tells me this is impossible.

Recently, an influential person in my life shared a harsh criticism of me which prompted me to write How To Deal With Criticism. While I didn't agree with his assessment of my abilities, I temporarily allowed his opinion to overshadow my belief in myself. The problem wasn't that I believed he was right in his opinion. The problem was that I feared continued criticism, and for a short time, I allowed this to hold me back.

Despite my fear of future criticism, I chose to believe in myself and keep doing my best. I refused to let anyone else's opinion of my work undermine my honest efforts and the great results that I know I can achieve.

HERE ARE A FEW WAYS TO BELIEVE IN YOURSELF, EVEN IF NO ONE ELSE BELIEVES IN YOU:

- Align your behavior with your values
- Align your choices with your intentions

- Discover other sources of support
- Tell yourself you can
- Always do your best
- Celebrate your accomplishments

Instead of making this excuse, commit yourself to believing in yourself. Other people's opinions shouldn't matter. Everyone has a different set of perspectives and experiences that color the way they see the world. Moreover, people judge you and your ability very differently. At times they will simply doubt you because they themselves don't understand something or don't believe it is possible. What is impossible for them doesn't have to be impossible for you. You have a different set of skills, knowledge and experiences that can help you bring your dreams into reality.

DOUBLE CHECK YOUR MOTIVES

it is true that "actions speak louder than words" and that "behind every action, there is a motive." A motive is something (a thought or a feeling) that makes you act in a certain way. With an honest approach and self-reflection, you can authentically determine what your motives are behind every action. Why should you check your motives? Because motives can set you up for success or failure, happiness or despair.

You can very easily hinder your success if your motives are driven by selfishness. On the contrary, if your motives are driven by prudence and honesty, you will experience positive outcomes. You should constantly practice evaluating your motives and be open and willing to be completely honest with yourself as to why you are choosing to take certain actions like the following for examples:

Seeking the approval of others is one major motive that some people are driven by to feel confident. This is something that will drain you emotionally and produce emptiness and disappointment in your life.

In the pursuit to gain the approval of others, you keep saying yes to people when they ask for favors, even when your schedule is already overloaded.

This becomes an unhealthy habit that instead of helping you feel confident, it will make you feel disappointed, hopeless and even depressed.

Boasting about your-self is an underlying action that is driven by a motive of arrogance and self-centeredness. Far from bringing more people into your life, you will be alienating them. This is not the right approach to gaining admiration.

Admiration is earned by pure motives like respecting people, doing good for others and being true to your-self. It is much more rewarding to be praised by others than to praise your-self, let others do it. Although, a sense of healthy pride is fine.

USING ENVIRONMENTAL EXCUSES

if you do not like to be a rabbit then change it. you are the master of your destiny. do not blame your enviroment, you can't you them as an excuse for not attainng your gals. that's the game of losers and cowards.

never blame outside factors, never say what could if....you need to foucus only on what you can do now with all your assets. you need to bring out the best as much as possible from your current, existing knowledge, assets.

economy, politics, weather, your neighbour, etc..it is easy to blame these factors for your failure, but believe it or not these factors influence also your competition not only you.

you can not change these factors, just as you can not change the politics. you need to accept them, acknowledge the rules and go forward towards your aims. sitting and waitng for the changes is equal with suicide because you will lose the control over things

To get the reason that no-one can do that for you. You cannot use outsourcing for courage than another person. It's a function of your personal commitment. Therefore, any result you labor and birth is a function of how you nurture the circumstances around you. All of us might spend another few of days fully coping with more of these external excuses we create to feed mediocrity. This kind of is an chance to claim back the right over your life. I celebrate your courage to intentionally lead your life daily.

I DON'T HAVE ANY ONE TO HELP ME

People who don't support you and discourage you may not actually be bad people who intentionally want to destroy your dreams. Sometimes, they just don't understand why you do what you do, so they voice out their concerns, which may make them seem dissenting.

I personally try not to take it to heart when people didn't help me. I see it as they need a little education and explanation. Or sometimes, I just ignore them. If anything, since they don't fully understand, I don't see why it's something to be upset over.

Sometimes when people don't support what you're doing, it may be more about them than you. It could be plain ignorance or even jealousy, but some people tend to attack things that are new to them.

So again, don't take their words to heart. If their criticism isn't constructive in any way, they may be discouraging you because of their own fears and insecurities.

Nobody can predict the future for certain.

The people who don't support you might paint a gloomy picture of what's to come if you do what you want to do. You don't know the future either, but do you want to listen to others instead of believing in yourself?

Don't let objections from others become your truth and limit you from creating what you want in life. Anything is possible if you believe in yourself and work hard.

It's natural to want support and encouragement from the people around you, but it is possible to do what you want to do without it. Just think of how many successful, inspiring people took the road less traveled.

You're a very powerful being, just by yourself. Believe in that, don't give up, and you'll go a long way, whichever road you take.

THE ECONOMY IS VERY BAD

Stop complaining about the economy. Protect Your Mindset! Most of the financial news is really negative. And if you don't block it out and focus on doing the few things that will generate profits and successful results, you'll start the downward spiral into bankruptcy.

I can guarantee that finding success, despite the economic environment, won't be easy. At times it will be like swimming upstream, but it can be done. Salmon do it every year because they know the reward they'll receive when they get there (I'm talking about the survival of the species!). It will be exhausting, but if you can avoid making excuses and continually focus on what needs to be done to meet your objectives, you will succeed.

As you embark on this journey to success, you will constantly be faced with roadblocks. With each one you must ask yourself, "What must I do now to still meet my goals?" The game plan will need to be adjusted with each new challenge. But if you face each new dilemma with the belief that there are no excuses and you must find a way to prevail, you will. If you don't meet your goals, it's not because of the economy. It's because you didn't do everything necessary to succeed. If you don't believe that, you've already failed.

Great people make a great nation not the other way round. If you are the onlyone that can align yourself with prosperity, then you better stop blaming theeconomy. Start creating your economy.

I DON'T HAVE ENOUGH KNOWLEDGE

"We Can't All Be Brilliant But We Can All Be Excellent"

I'm just not educated enough.
I just don't have enough knowledge.

Why bother to be excellent? Because we are happiest if we are. The Lord knows that from experience. He is most excellent (perfect), and he wants us all to be like him. For us right now, excellence doesn't mean perfection, but it means to be traveling toward perfection at full speed. Many of us, unfortunately, are not even in gear, though we know well where the road is. A primary symptom of lack of excellence in college students is excuse-making.

Maybe you don't have internet, not everyone does (how are you reading this?)

In any case, there are these buildings with a number of books on a variety of subjects called libraries. They'll be thrilled to see you, and eager to help. If you invest the time, a near college level education awaits you. No it's not as convenient as the internet, but learning anything worthwhile is seldom easy. Also reading books will help to fortify your attention span, which is vital to your success.

There's one word kicks this excuse right in the teeth.

"Google."

If you can't find a ton of free information on Google, find a book on Amazon.If Amazon doesn't work, hire a coach. Information is more accessible now than any other point in history, and most of it is free.
Spend time to find it, Commit to learning it and Be equipped to tackle your challenge.

Instead of making this excuse, commit yourself to growth and development. If you don't have enough knowledge about something, then read some books or chat with someone who can provide you with the guidance you need in this area. Knowledge is everywhere, and for the most part it is free. You just need to commit yourself to going out there and securing it for yourself.

I HAVE NO MONEY

"If only I had the money"

One of the most common excuses.

The fact is that money should never stop you, whether it be having more adventures, doing something different or making your dreams come true. It costs less than you think if you are willing to make changes and be creative.

Finances are a sensitive issue. You might not have the money right now, but there are plenty of ways to increase your income. If you have to scour freelancer sites to a?uire a hundred dollars here and there, do it. Any money you make freelancing, save it to put towards your dream project.
Can't afford to do that?
Create a strict budget, and set aside a portion of your income. Don't believe what the news tells you, money is everywhere, and people spend it every day. Right now, someone is hiring someone just like you.

Ask around, it's amazing what friends and family will take off your hands. I offloaded all my high value items that I didn't want/didn't fit into my future lifestyle and managed to raise ?uite a lot of money, something I wouldn't have got by holding onto something that I didn't need.

You know what you want, your dream is burning a hole in your heart and you are holding yourself back from going for it 'cause you don't have enough capital?

Money is fun if and when we have it. It's fun to spend it on 'stuff'. And it's frustrating not to have it. Money is the one thing that makes the world go round. And don't let anyone tell you otherwise.

"I started my business without any money" is a lie! You can start a business without having any previous experiences- but without having money? Forget it!

It all depends on what kind of business you want to start, for sure. The home based solo-preneur saves on rent and municipality costs but still needs to invest in a computer, a website, a printer, paper, perhaps even in a copy writer, a web designer etc. These costs are less high than starting a brick and mortar business. Still, these are costs.

Here are a few ideas on how to come up with the cash you need to make your dream come true!

- Calculate exactly how much you need. List everything from rent, furniture, equipment, to daily/monthly running costs (be really conservative in your estimates)!

- Do a personal inventory of all your bank accounts (-savings-, daily-investment-accounts).

- How much money exactly is missing?

- List institutions and individuals from where the funds could be coming from!

- Check on government loans and grants for small businesses or newcomers! Are you eligible?

- Start your personal saving account, labelled 'dream-fund'!

- The big question is, what personal sacrifices are you willing to make? Are you willing to go out less, buy fewer clothes, less shoes, and go on less expensive trips? Would you downsize from your big car to a smaller one? Change your shopping habits at the supermarket? Shop at a less expensive supermarket even?

- Brainstorm ideas on how to earn extra money: Do you have time for a second job? Could you rent out your second room? Could you bike to work instead of driving? Carpooling? Eat at home, eating out? Sell unwanted clothes at a flea market / garage sale?

- Be careful and selective who of your family members and friends you could trust asking for a loan!

And last but not least, a few words about banks:

- Banks normally give loans to individuals who can offer a guarantee or guarantor.

- They also want to see how much personal investment you have.

- Loans specific to your field might be available.

- Rates vary, compare banks.

All in all, it is not impossible to gather your start–up capital together. Keep your eyes and ears open, become creative and make personal sacrifices! And you will be one step closer to your dream!

Money should never ever stop you from reaching your goals, you always have choice and more choice than you think. It all boils down to how much you want it. Are you ready to be creative or strip away the crap you don't need?

I AM AFRAID OF MAKING MISTAKES

I'm afraid of making a mistake.

I'm reluctant because I might goof this up.

Instead of making this excuse, accept the fact that mistakes are a natural part of life. We all make mistakes. In fact, no matter how much experience someone has, they are still be prone to making mistakes. Mistakes are however valuable as they help you learn and grow from the experience. In fact, making mistakes is a natural part of success. As long as you take the time to learn from these mistakes, they can lead to tremendous growth opportunities and insights that can help you move forward in a better way.

Many people out there have intense fear of making mistakes.

Those people don't just find it hard to fail or to make a mistake but they also suffer from a low self esteem as a result of their way of thinking.

All humans make mistakes and thus if someone believed that making a mistake makes him less worthy than others then each and every day his self confidence will go lower as the result of the mistakes he makes.

xliv

But why do some people find it really shameful to make a mistake while others consider it a part of the human nature?

The difference between the two groups lies in their belief system and in the way they have been treated when they were children.

Because such negative beliefs about making mistakes can lower your self confidence i decided to write this article to tell you how to overcome the fear of making mistakes.

UNDERSTANDING THE FEAR OF MAKING MISTAKES

If you want to overcome the fear of making mistakes then you must first examine your belief system to find out whether you have any of the following negative beliefs:

I can learn without making mistakes: Do you know how learning happens? its a process of continuously making mistakes and adjusting your methods until you no longer make mistakes. No wonder people who think that mistaking is shameful have a low self esteem for they never give themselves the chance to develop a new skill that can make them feel good about themselves:

Its shameful to make a mistake: In the Solid Self confidence program i said that when people are brought up to believe that making mistakes is a shameful act they lose their self confidence when they grow up because the human nature always forces them to make mistakes. This belief is usually learned when the parents shout at the little kid or embarrass him in public when he makes a mistake. At this point the child starts to believe that its too shameful to make a mistake.

So how to overcome the fear of making mistakes?

In order to overcome the fear of making mistakes you must understand that mistaking is an essential step for learning.

Because you will never be able to develop a new skill without passing through the learning phase you will never be able to reach anything before you make some mistakes!

Do you know why some people want to avoid mistakes? its because they believe that they are less worthy than others and as a result they want to hide their flaws by never drawing the attention to them!

In such a case a person believes that the best way to hide his flaws is to appear as perfect as he can and this is where perfectionism comes from.

Perfectionism is just a defense mechanism that some people who don't feel good about themselves use to hide their flaws!

In short if you want to overcome the fear of making mistakes you must understand that mistaking is a normal part of the human nature.

I JUST DON'T HAVE LUCK

I just don't have any luck.

I have the worst rotten bad luck of anyone I know.

Our reliance on luck is everywhere. Lotteries thrive. Investors and their advisors treat the stock markets like great casinos, playing secret strategies that rival those at the roulette tables. Jobseekers send out hundreds of résumés randomly, hoping that one of them will be a perfect fit.

People use luck as an excuse, but I don't think it's entirely an excuse, part of it relies on a person's intuition and, perhaps view in life. I personally believe in luck, and it kind of affects everything I do, if I may say so. Family, work, friends, poker, it plays a big part of my life, to be just an 'excuse'.

Luck has even invaded our language. We continue to wish each other good luck for every possible occasion, from exams to job interviews to investments. Perhaps you might conclude that this incessant wishing of good luck is no more than a social convention. But conventions reflect a widespread societal belief.

Instead of making this excuse, come to accept that luck increases as you take more chances, as you work harder, and as you network relentlessly with other people. The more people you know, the more opportunities you will be able to take advantage of. Moreover, those who are fearless and courageously take bold steps toward their goal, end up experiencing far more good fortune than anyone else. After all, you're never going to win a race if you never get off the starting line.

I HAVE A DISABILITY

Josh Blue is a hilarious stand up comic with cerebral palsy, which most noticeably affects his right arm.

Nick Vujicic is a world-renowned preacher and motivational speaker who doesn't have any arms or legs.

Kyle Maynard doesn't have arms or legs either, and is a wrestler, MMA fighter, owner of a gym, a student, and a motivational speaker. Oh, and he's 25 years old.

I'm 33 and have a rare brain condition, and I'm supporting my family and growing my business.

There are artists who create with their mouths, runners who win races on artificial legs, brilliant writers who's fingers never touch the keyboard and a host of successful individuals with learning, cognitive, and emotional disabilities who refuse to let their situation hold them back.

"If you're not willing to be uncomfortable, you're not willing to succeed."

If you're someone that makes comments like:

- I can't do that. I'm an introvert.

- The event sounds awesome, but you know me, the introvert.

- I wish I could, but I'm not great around people.

- That's too uncomfortable. Wouldn't work for me.

Cut that shit out. Now. Today. Get out there and be uncomfortable. But more importantly, get out there and be free. Don't let excuses and discomfort stop you from being great. Don't get trapped in yourself. Go to a relevant networking event or conference where you know there are people with similar interests, and push yourself to stay away from the wall. (Bring your extroverted friend with you need be necessary.) Hell, create your own event and ask friends to each invite a couple positive people. Control the numbers. Start a Meetup group. Make use of sites like Facebook, Twitter, and LinkedIn to warm up relationships. Email people! Consider opportunities for public speaking (my work in progress)!

There are so many things you can do to break out of your comfort zone. And once you start doing them, you'll be surprised at the results: new contacts, friends, and opportunities. But the best part to me is no longer feeling like a slave to something you think no one else gets.

It's time to take control. It's time to be free. Not a slave to a mentality. Get out there and get uncomfortable!

Some people use disability as an excuse but the truth is that disability is NOT inability. If you are disabled in some way this does not mean that you are unable, just that you have certain limitations that must be worked around. Anyone who does not want to be productive and contribute to society will find a reason not to do so, and those who are truly disabled tend to find ways to work around their limitations instead of letting their disability define them and what they can do. Even those who are truly disabled in severe ways can still offer their knowledge and the abilities that they still maintain to the world. Look at Stephen Hawking and everything that he has managed to do in spite of being in a wheelchair and having very limited movement.

If you have a disability of some type do not let this stop you from trying to achieve your goals. We all have restrictions and limitations. Some are physical, some are mental, and some are emotional. The point is that no one has a perfect life and there is an enormous difference between being disabled and being unable to accomplish something. No matter what disability you have look at the situation and determine what you hope to achieve, and then create a plan to make it happen. Some of the best moments in life happen when you do something that everyone tells you is impossible. If you let a disability hold you back then you are missing out on one of the best experiences life offers.

THERE ARE TOO MANY OBSTACLES

I just can't deal with all these problems.

There are just too many things getting in my way.

Tell me one epic story in which the protagonist doesn't overcome too many obstacles.

To save the princess, you must travel the land, sail the ocean, answer the riddles of the old man at the bridge, and bring an offering to the king.

Only then can you slay the dragon.

It's going to be difficult, but trust me, the princess (your freedom) is worth it.

"Until" is the worst word you can allow into your vocabulary when it comes to your goals because it gives you a free pass to avoid taking action. It's easy to say you can't get to something "until" something changes, like your finances, or your schedule, or some other external circumstance.

For example, it's easy to say "I can't start losing weight until I can get to (or afford) the gym," or "until I can figure out a solid meal plan." In this case, you're naming something as an obstacle – it's

liv

either time, money or information. You use this obstacle as an excuse, and you give it permission to roadblock your progress.

I say you "give it permission" because the very act of acknowledging this circumstance as an obstacle means you're saying it's okay for this to be a significant road-block to your goals.

And once you give the "all clear" to the obstacle, it's unlikely you'll work very hard to change your circumstances. That's not a knock against you, it's just human nature. It's just the way it is. If something gives you an easy way out, you're likely to take it if you haven't conditioned yourself to push back against it.

This is especially true if we're afraid of the true cost of taking action – maybe we don't think we're strong enough, or we're just not sure where to start and the effort seems overwhelming. And because we don't see how we're going to finish on our desired timetable, we don't see the point in starting.

Instead of making this excuse, treat everything as a learning experience. Remember that adversity often leads to growth and development. The more adversity you face the more you'll learn and the wiser you'll become on your next attempt. As long as you keep an open mind and stay flexible in thought and action, you will eventually breakthrough and then wonder how on earth you didn't figure all this out earlier.

I DON'T WANT TO TAKE A RISK

If not now, then when?

This excuse is fear of the unknown.

The reality is, you can't afford not to take a risk right now.

If an idea really benefits people, pulling on the reigns doesn't just inhibit your progress...it prevents people from improving their lives.

"Fear is inevitable, I have to accept that, but I cannot allow it to paralyze me." ~Isabelle Allende

Instead of making this excuse, remind yourself that fortune favors the brave. Yes, all risks don't always payoff, but if you never take a chance on yourself then you will never really know how far you can go. Too many people don't live up to their full potential simply because they never step away from the confines of their comfort zone. Everything you want is there for the taking, however you must have the courage and guts to go after it. At the end of the day you will always regret the things you didn't do more than the things you did.

You think Neil and Buzz weren't freaking out before they got into an eight-ton firecracker that was going to take three days to get to the moon? They didn't even know if they'd sink elbow deep in moon dust, but they took one small step for man, and an even greater leap for mankind.

I am sure that despite the years of preparation and endless simulations, they still had a sleepless night before one of humanity's biggest risks.

Most people who take risks are kidding themselves if they don't doubt themselves a teeny tiny bit. So do yourself a favor and take one small step toward your goal despite your apprehensions and gut-wrenching fear.

FAKE IT UNTIL YOU MAKE IT

Like I did, and so many other risk takers do, you have to fake it until you make it. It sounds cliché but it holds a boatload of truth. Use reverse psychology on yourself. You're your own worst enemy. Tell yourself and others that you are confident about taking the risk and notice how your apprehension will dissolve.

NURTURE THE POSITIVES, NOT THE FEAR
Print out some pictures of your risk and tape them on your ceiling so when you wake up with cold sweats, you can remind yourself that you are going to do what it is that you set out to do. I put pictures

of Patagonia as my desktop screensaver to remind me of the beauty I would experience in Argentina.

Write a pros list and forget the cons. Focus on the major pros. Cons can always be worked through.

Whether it is lack of money, not knowing the language, being thousands of miles away from home, I knew that it was what I had always wanted to do and I could find money by selling all my things, or start learning basic phrases or use Skype to talk to friends and family. There is a positive to every negative.

I AM NOT CREATIVE ENOUGH

If you believe you're "Just not the creative type", there's no point even trying to think or act creatively. You'd just be setting yourself up for failure.

Forget about who you are (or think you are) and what qualities you may or may not have.
Forget nouns ('creativity', 'creation', 'creator') and adjectives ('creative'), and focus on verbs ('create', 'creating'). In other words, stop worrying about theories, and start taking action.
And whatever you do, consign the thought "I'm not creative" to the dustbin. It's meaningless, useless, and doesn't suit you at all. Take a moment to listen to the Thud! as it lands in the bottom of the bin, and the Clang! as you slam the lid shut on top of it.
You might even like to take five minutes to watch the garbage collectors empty the bin into their truck, and motor off into the distance, on their way to dump it in the landfill of all the limiting and unhelpful beliefs that human beings have no more use for.

I'm just not creative enough to figure this out.

Creativity just isn't my strength.

Instead of making this excuse, accept the fact that creativity is often a numbers gain. For every 100 bad ideas you generate, you will see a return of ONE good idea. Given this, commit yourself to generating as many ideas as possible. In fact, spend time brainstorming with others. Two minds are always better than one. Use other people's ideas to help stimulate your own imagination to help you come up with something that will allow you to move forward in a more optimal way.

But even with all this in mind, creativity isn't always necessary. Overcoming problems doesn't require creativity. Persistence, perseverance, determination and passion often trump even the most creative of ideas.

I AM TOO YOUNG / TOO OLD

Stop saying you are too young or too old. its never too late…you are never too young to achieve your dreams…if you think otherwise, then check out those who has surpassed the mindset of being too old or too young…

- Mozart was eight when he wrote his first symphony.
- Anne Frank was thirteen when she began her diary.
- Ralph Waldo Emerson was fourteen when he enrolled at Harvard.
- Bill Gates was nineteen when he cofounded Microsoft.
- Henry David Thoreau was twenty-seven when he moved to Walden Pond, built a house, planted a garden, and began a two-year experiment in simplicity and self-reliance.
- Bill Gates was thirty-one when he became a billionaire.
- Thomas Jefferson was thirty-three when he wrote the Declaration of Independence.
- Coco Chanel was thirty-eight when she introduced her perfume Chanel No. 5.

- Mother Teresa was forty when she founded the Missionaries of Charity.
- Henry Ford was fifty when he started his first manufacturing assembly line.
- Ray Kroc was fifty-two when he started McDonalds.
- Dom Perignon was sixty when he produced his first champagne.
- Oscar Hammerstein II was sixty-four when he wrote the lyrics for The Sound of Music.
- Winston Churchill was sixty-five when he became Britain's prime minister.
- Nelson Mandela was seventy-one when he was released from a South African prison, and seventy-five when he was elected president.

It does not matter how old or young you are. never use age as an excuse. using age as an excuse is one of the worst kinds of negative thinking you can have. saying to yourself "i am too young to do this" or i am too old to do this" is a crazy thinking. i hear it all the time. i see it in people's eyes and on their faces when i talkj to them. you are never too old or too young to change your perspective and your thinking to positive. put the book down again and tell yourself that. go ahead, put it down. close your eyes and tell yourself that you are never too young or too old to become a positive person. then write it down on your piece of paper..you have to do it now!

I HAVE TRIED MY BEST. NO ONE IS PERFECT

Every time I hear somebody say, "But nobody is perfect!" I cringe. Why? Because most of the time, they are looking at the imperfect lives of others and using the weaknesses of others to excuse some sin or issue in their own life. This behavior is not found in scripture... as a matter of fact, we are never to excuse sin or weakness, but rather put the light on the wrong, and get it dealt with. The sooner we get things made right, the better off we will be. Let's stop looking at the problem and excusing it, and let's ask ourselves a very valuable question: Why are we not perfect? Why do we struggle in certain areas of our lives? Because there are strongholds (incorrect thinking patterns... spider webs in our mind), unclean spirits (which can make it very difficult for a person to resist sin), or we are still allowing other things to become more important to us than our relationship with God (lack of relationship with God).

Saying that nobody is perfect puts a serious damper on God's ability to transform us... it turns a positive (our ability to become perfect) into a negative (we'll never be perfect).

Let's face it, none of us are perfect. Whether you are a young Christian or someone seasoned in the faith, we make mistakes. Every day. I think one of the biggest issues I have with older Christians is that, sometimes they think they are above everyone else--like they've been saved, sanctified and Holy Ghost filled every single day of their lives. Now, I don't know everyone' s life story, but I know no one is free from sin and mistakes. But it isn't the mistake so much that creates the problem--it's our actions following the mistakes that we are held accountable for.

We fear less and become FEARLESS in situations when we don't have all of the information and answers. We cease to struggle with the emotion attached to perfection. Yes, perfection is an emotion, as well as a goal we experience and attempt to achieve. The pursuit of excellence requires fearlessness and imperfection. Is anyone ever really 100% ready for everything?

THE FOLLOWING WAYS WILL LET YOU GET OVER IMPERFECTION....

1) SET REALISTIC GOALS AND EXPECTATIONS. Don't tell someone you will be able to complete your task in one day when you have a bunch of other tasks you are working on. Always give yourself at least a day or two of room when setting deadlines to avoid late nights and too much caffeine.

2) GO WITH YOUR GUT. There is no such thing as a perfect choice yet we spend so much time agonizing over perfection with our decisions. Sometimes the decisions you have to go with are just good enough. Try to gain about 80% of the information you need from mentors and research and then make a decision.

3) GIVE YOURSELF AN INTERNAL DEADLINE. Make internal deadlines for when you need to move onto other task so you don't spend all day trying to make one project perfect. If you haven't completely finished the current task, move onto the next task and settle for as good as can be in the time available. If you need to, you can always return to the task at a later time with a fresh perspective.

4) ASK FOR AN EXTENSION. I know, it's hard because asking for an extension shows that you aren't perfect. But, usually there is no negative side effect for asking for an extension because it shows that you really care. (Just don't make a habit of constantly missing deadlines, which can ultimately ruin your trust and reputation. Make sure you know the difference between a hard deadline and a soft deadline.)

5) AIM FOR BEING RESPECTED INSTEAD OF BEING LIKED. This simple change in your mindset can really help you eliminate your desire to be perfect. This

comes back to our female characteristic of wanting everyone to like us. We need to get past this because not everyone is going to like us at work. Instead, strive for having the people you work with respect you. This is the most important thing. Look for respect instead of trying to be a people pleaser.

We are all imperfect and trying to get to perfect can come with a lot of stress. I challenge you to use these five tips and stop giving excuse on your imperfection..you will then see how much happier and less stressed you become.

I'M TOO BUSY..I DONT HAVE ENOUGH TIME

"It's not always that you have more to do, but if those things seem like they're in conflict—even when the source of the conflict is unrelated to time—you can still get the feeling of being time-constrained," says Etkin.

Too many of us seek out busyness for the sake of being busy, says Etkin.

"As a culture, we hate being idle and we value productivity, but there is a growing movement toward mindfulness and savoring," she says. *"You have a lot to gain from not being busy all the time. Step back and be peaceful. It doesn't have to be scary, and it can be enjoyable."*

Etkin says her most important takeaway from the study is that we're in control of our sense of time: "We sense a feeling that we're time-constrained, yet we're more time-affluent than we think we are," she says. "If we can manage our experience of time through interventions and conflict reduction, we can start to see that."

I promise, with this two-step process, you'll be able to deal with the problem of "too much to do, not enough time."

SIMPLIFY WHAT YOU DO

When we realize we're trying to fit too much stuff (tasks, errands, obligations) into a small container (24 hours), it becomes obvious that we can't get a bigger container … so we have to get rid of some stuff. It just won't all fit.

We do that by simplifying what we have to do.

Mindfulness is a helpful too here: pay attention to all the things you do today and tomorrow, and try to notice all the things you're fitting into the container of your day. What websites are you going to in the morning? In the evening? What games are you playing on your phone? What are you reading? What busy-work are you doing? How much time are you spending in email, on Facebook, on Twitter, on Instagram? How much time on blogs, online shopping sites, Youtube? How much TV are you watching? How much time do you spend cleaning, maintaining your personal hygiene, taking care of other people? How much time driving around or commuting? What are you spending the valuable commodity of your attention on?

By picking your tasks carefully, you're taking care with the container of your time. You can pick important tasks or joyful ones, but you're being conscious about the choices. You're treating it like the precious gift that it is: limited, valuable, to be filled with the best things, and not overstuffed.

THE ART OF LETTING GO

What about all the other stuff you want to do (or feel you need to do)? What if it doesn't fit into the container?

This is where the joyful art of letting go becomes useful.

You have too many things to fit into your container, and you've decided to only put the important and beautiful things into the container. That means a bunch of things you think you "should" do are not going to fit.

You can get to those later. Or you can not do them. Either way, they won't fit into today's container.

This in itself is not a problem, but it only becomes a problem when you are frustrated that you can't fit it all in. Your frustration comes from an ideal that you should be able to do it all, that you should be able to do everything on your list. Plus more: you want to travel, workout, meditate, learn a new skill, read more, be the perfect spouse (or find a spouse), be the perfect parent/friend/sibling, draw or create music, and so on.

To finish up, I want to reiterate. Everyone has the same amount of time. Figure out what is important to you (not others) and make that a priority. Spend a little time up front organizing your life and see how you can actually give yourself more free time in the long run.

In fact, you have all the time, resources, and knowledge re?uired to be great.

Being great, no, being excellent, is a choice.

It's a choice to never stop. It's a choice to view yourself as limitless. It's a choice to stop at nothing until everyone knows your name.

Without a doubt, you'll encounter many obstacles on your journey. That's a given.

So what are you waiting for?

Go.

Be great.

A lack of time is not the problem, wasting time and filling your life with unimportant things is the problem.

I DON'T KNOW WHERE TO START

I just don't know where to begin.

I have no idea where to start.

Instead of making this excuse, acknowledge that help and support from others can be of tremendous value. With this in mind, commit yourself to asking for help from someone who has knowledge and experience in this area. If by chance that person isn't available, then just start somewhere. Most people who just get started eventually work things out as they move along their journey toward a goal. In fact, the more you do, the more you'll know exactly what needs to get done.

The human brain isn't designed to process information in a linear fashion.

This is why when you dream, it doesn't start "at the beginning" and you only remember how the dream ended, but never how it began.

If you're looking to pick up a new skill, usually "the beginning" will make itself apparent, regardless of where you start.

Even better, because the way you process information is unique to you, your "starting point" could help you form a very unique perspective that people love.

Also consider the other people who "don't know where to begin."

By simply picking a place and chronicling your journey, you can inspire others to learn with you.

THINGS ARE TOO HARD FOR ME

This is all just too hard.

I'm just not good enough.

Anything worth doing is hard.

When was the last time "easy" had a huge payoff for you?

Instead of making this excuse, accept the fact that learning something new takes time, energy and effort. Often, the greater the difficulty of a task the higher reward and satisfaction you will gain from accomplishing it. With this in mind, challenge yourself to do better on each attempt. Alternatively you could always outsource difficult tasks or find a partner with complementary skills who could help you out. Mentors can also be of value to help guide you through a difficult challenge.

I FEAR FAILURE WOULD CRUSH ME

I fear failure would absolutely crush me.

I'm afraid of looking and feeling like a failure.

Instead of making this excuse, acknowledge the fact that failure is only a temporary experience, unless of course you accept defeat. If you choose not to accept defeat, then failure becomes nothing more than feedback. It becomes a learning experience that helps you adjust your course of action moving forward. In fact, failure can very often contain the seeds of an opportunity. But of course this opportunity is never handed to you on a silver platter. You must do the work to figure out how to make the most of every experience.

Anyone who has ever made it, will tell you they've failed more times than they've succeeded.

Being destroyed by failure is a choice; the choice is to quit.

If you fail, fail.

Give it everything you've got, and let it become a disaster.

Watch it burn.Let it destroy you.

lxxvi

Then recoup, learn from your mistakes, and rise from the ashes.

Failure never completely destroys you, only the parts that weren't doing you any good.

With every catastrophic failure, hindsight allows you to see where you went wrong.

When you rebuild, you're that much closer to perfecting the system.

YOU HAVEN'T DONE IT BEFORE

This is my favorite excuse, because it's such a cop out.

Let's look at some of the common milestones in your life that you got through just fine

- You went to school (hadn't done that before)
- Had your first kiss (hadn't done that before)
- Learned to drive a car
- Took up a new hobby
- Learned to read

Or really anything beyond lying on your back and flailing your limbs uncontrollably.

You hadn't done anything before you did it. It's simple, but it's true.

This excuse is rooted in fear of the unknown.

Now it's perfectly fine to be afraid, but "inexperience" is by far one of the worst excuses.

Life is built on a series of "firsts" and making the choice to limit your experiences only leads to dissatisfaction.

YOU'LL GET TO IT LATER.

No you won't. You never do.

Get to it now, or at least schedule it to get done.

Then do it.

You'll be a lot more satisfied when you're finished.

You don't want to be boring.

What's boring to some is addictive to others.

People process information differently. If you skew towards boring it's entirely possible to still find the right audience.

However if you skew towards boring, and you don't want to, find ways to become more interesting.

Take an improvise class, do some live Q&A's, go bungee jumping... spice it up.

NOT ENOUGH CONFIDENCE

I'm just not confident enough to do this.

I don't have the confidence to make this work.

Instead of making this excuse, acknowledge that self-confidence comes with competence and experience. It's perfectly okay to lack confidence when you are doing something for the very first time. Familiarity breeds confidence. In other words, the more you know about something, the more familiar you become and the more confidence you develop in yourself and in your own ability. And if in doubt, just Act As If you're already confident.

IF I SUCCEED, MY RESPONSIBILITIES WILL CHANGE.

Not only to your customers, but to your personal life as well.

This isn't a bad thing.

New responsibilities that improve people's lives is a good thing.

Remember, it comes incrementally. It's up to decide when to say yes and when to say no.

But don't not do something because you don't think you can handle the responsibility.

Give it a shot.

If it doesn't work, be responsible to enough to find a suitable replacement.

I DON'T WANT TO SPEND TOO MUCH TIME AWAY FROM MY FAMILY.

This is another one of those really sensitive excuses.

Obviously (hopefully) if you have a family, you don't want to leave them for long periods of time.

If you can, make arrangements for them to come with you, or find ways to attend long distance events virtually.

If virtual isn't an option, be sure to keep an open line of communication, and make every effort to stay connected.

When you return home, commit to distraction free family time.

Explore all of your options, and don't hide behind your family as an excuse to get out of something you don't want to do.

You can't until you have.........

Money, desk, tools, website, secretary, bank account, more influence or any other number of outside factors.

lxxxii

Make every attempt to acquire the bare essentials quickly.

Plot out your steps and create milestones.

Missions and objectives do wonders for progress.

BONUS

YOU'RE TOO TIRED.

Put yourself on a schedule, structure your day, and get more rest.

If necessary (and possible) take naps when you can, and remain productive.

Productivity sparks energy.

If you're chronically tired, improve your fitness, and increase your vitamin intake.

Sometimes a vitamin supplement is necessary, and sometimes you need to suck it up and get it done.

YOU DID EVERYTHING YOU COULD

Did you really?

Did you see where you went wrong?

Try again.

Who knows, you might be successful next time.

MOTIVATIONAL QUOTES TO PONDER

Don't look for excuses to lose. Look for excuses to win. – Chi Chi Rodriguez

Don't use your past as an excuse, excuse your excuses and take action now! — Bernard Kelvin Clive

Don't you dare take the lazy way. It's too easy to excuse yourself because of your ancestry. Don't let me catch you doing it! Now — look close at me so you will remember. Whatever you do, it will be you who do. — John Steinbeck

Difficulty on the way to victory is opportunity for God to work. – Henry Wadsworth Longfellow

Pessimism is an excuse for not trying and a guarantee to a personal failure. – Bill Clinton

He that is good for making excuses is seldom good for anything else. – Benjamin Franklin

Hold yourself responsible for a higher standard than anybody else expects of you, never excuse yourself. – Henry Ward Beecher

If you don't want to do something, one excuse is as good as another. – Yiddish Proverb

People are always blaming their circumstances for what they are. I don't believe in circumstances. The people who get on in this world are the people who get up and look for the circumstances they want, and, if they can't find them, make them. – George Bernard Shaw

CONCLUSION

So there you have it... the 30 days no excuse challenges that will change your life forever.

Indulging in these excuses will often keep you stuck. They are very much self-sabotaging forces that prevent us from moving forward with our lives. In fact, they hold us back from achieving our goals by keeping us within the confines of our comfort zones.

Awareness is of course the first step to change. Becoming aware of your excuses and subduing them before they take over your mind is the key to developing new habitual thinking patterns.

With time and practice you will get better at turning these excuses into positive proactive action that will help you move closer toward your desired goals and objectives.

DISCLAIMER

Although the author and publisher have made every effort to ensure that the information in this book was correct at press time, the author and publisher do not assume and hereby disclaim any liability to any party for any loss, damage, or disruption caused by errors or omissions, whether such errors or omissions result from negligence, accident, or any other cause.

DO NOT GO YET; ONE LAST THING TO DO

If you enjoyed this book or found it useful I'd be very grateful if you'd post a short review on Amazon. Your support really does make a difference and I read all the reviews personally so I can get your feedback and make this book even better.

Please, please, please...

Thanks again for your support!

ABOUT THE AUTHOR

I write books that help people. Some people like my no-nonsense, step by step, no fluff books. Some people don't. Others are offended with my "non-professional" - "non-traditional" writer voice.

Growing up in a small town in North Carolina, William always had big dreams of making an impact in the world. William enlisted into the U.S. Army where he knew his leadership and mentorship would be put to the test on a daily bases.

After graduating college and retiring from the U.S. Army, William continued with his life's purpose of: "Making a thunderous dent in the environment and world around him. To infect millions of people, with purpose, direction, and motivation. To achieve "The Good Life" in four areas: health, wealth, love, and happiness. William is determined to follow his passion for coaching and mentoring. So read my books with discretion.

53878435R00053

Made in the USA
Middletown, DE
01 December 2017